Just Add Sugar to Make

LEMONADE

Transform Anxiety Into Positivity

WHITNEY COLEMAN, LICSW, LCSW-C

Introduction

Welcome,

Writing your thoughts, feelings, and experiences in a journal is a great way to reduce stress and anxiety. Studies show that journaling helps to treat anxiety, depression, PTSD, and other conditions. It's especially helpful for people who struggle with cognitive distortions such as catastrophizing, overgeneralization, and all-or-nothing thinking. Journaling helps you challenge yourself when you are thinking negatively. When you list evidence supporting and contradicting your thoughts, it allows you to think more objectively. It can also help reduce intrusive thoughts and avoidant behaviors. Additionally, research suggests that writing about positive experiences can reduce symptoms of depression.

This journal is designed to be used daily over the course of a month to focus on the positive aspects of your life and build new habits. Each week, there's a session to review how things went and set intentions for the upcoming week.

A journey of a thousand miles begins with a decision. Your decision to focus on positivity can help you reduce depressive and anxious symptomology that occur in your life.

Be in Peace,

Whitney Coleman, LICSW, LCSW-C

"The goal isn't to get rid of all your negative thoughts and feelings; that's impossible. The goal is to change your response to them" - Unknown

Instructions

This workbook is here to help you understand anxiety, build helpful habits, and learn ways to manage your feelings. Over the next month, you'll take small steps to feel more in control. Each section will guide you from learning about anxiety to using practical tools to handle it. By the end, you'll have a personal plan to manage stress and find calm when you need it.

Each week focuses on something new:
- Week 1 helps you understand anxiety and where it comes from.
- Week 2 introduces simple techniques, like mindfulness and grounding, to help you feel calm.
- Week 3 is about shifting anxious thoughts and practicing self-compassion.
- Week 4 brings it all together by helping you track progress and build a plan to keep moving forward.

You'll find daily reflection pages to check in with yourself and notice patterns in your thoughts. Each week ends with an activity to practice what you've learned.

To help you build better habits, this workbook includes two habit trackers—one for focusing on a single habit for 30 days and another for tracking multiple habits throughout the month. Choose whichever works best for you (or use both!).

There's also a special "Dear Future Me" section where you'll write a letter to yourself. This is your chance to reflect on your journey and encourage yourself to keep going.

Anxiety doesn't have to control your life. Every small step you take matters. This workbook will help you find what works for you, at your own pace. Don't forget to utilize the free online course companion which has an additional activity book. The QR code is below. You've got this!

Self Assessment

- [ ]
- [ ]
- [ ]
- [ ]
- [ ]
- [ ]
- [ ]
- [ ]
- [ ]
- [ ]
- [ ]

- [ ]
- [ ]
- [ ]
- [ ]
- [ ]
- [ ]
- [ ]
- [ ]
- [ ]
- [ ]
- [ ]

I am proud of myself because...

_____
_____
_____

Something that makes me happy is...

_____
_____
_____

FILL EACH DAY WITH

DATE :

Positivity

BREATHE BEFORE WRITING...

INHALE EXHALE INHALE EXHALE INHALE EXHALE

WHAT ARE 3 GOOD THINGS WHICH HAPPENED TODAY?

WHAT POSITIVITY DID I PUT OUT INTO THE WORLD TODAY?

WHAT IS MY FAVORITE MOMENT OF THE DAY?

> "The only limit to our realization of tomorrow will be our doubts of today."
> - Franklin D. Roosevelt

WHAT ARE 3 SMALL THINGS I APPRECIATED TODAY?

WHAT ARE MY WINS FOR TODAY?

DESCRIBE TODAY IN 1 WORD.

WHAT ARE MY GOALS FOR TOMORROW?

FILL EACH DAY WITH

DATE :

Positivity

BREATHE BEFORE WRITING...

INHALE EXHALE INHALE EXHALE INHALE EXHALE

WHAT ARE 3 GOOD THINGS WHICH HAPPENED TODAY?

WHAT POSITIVITY DID I PUT OUT INTO THE WORLD TODAY?

WHAT IS MY FAVORITE MOMENT OF THE DAY?

"You are never too old to set another goal or to dream a new dream."
- Les Brown

WHAT ARE 3 SMALL THINGS I APPRECIATED TODAY?

WHAT ARE MY WINS FOR TODAY?

DESCRIBE TODAY IN 1 WORD.

WHAT ARE MY GOALS FOR TOMORROW?

Week 1: Understanding Anxiety and Mental Health
To Build Awareness and Knowledge

Mental Health Terms to Help You Understand Yourself Better

Talking about mental health can feel overwhelming, especially when clinical terms get thrown around like you're at the doctor's office. But understanding these words can make a huge difference. They help us describe what we're feeling and give us tools to get started on our mental health journey. Let's break down some common words you might have heard.

Anxiety disorder is a term you may be familiar with, but it's more than just feeling nervous before a test or big event. Anxiety disorders are when fear and worry stick around all the time and make everyday life harder. It's like your brain's alarm system is stuck in the "on" position, even when there's no real danger.

This is where cognitive-behavioral therapy (CBT) comes into play. CBT teaches you how to notice those anxious thoughts, challenge them, and replace them with more helpful ones.

Some terms describe patterns of thinking or behaviors that can make mental health challenges feel more difficult. For example, cognitive distortions are like tricks your brain plays on you. You might assume the worst (catastrophizing) or think in extremes (black-and-white thinking). Rumination is when you replay the same thought over and over. These thought patterns are common, and knowing what they are can help you recognize them and take steps to manage them.

Other terms describe how you react to stress or trauma. For instance, the fight-or-flight response is your body's way of protecting you. It's great when there's real danger, but it can also kick in during everyday stress, making you feel tense. Hypervigilance is a state of being constantly on high alert, as if waiting for something bad to happen. These responses don't mean that something is wrong with you; your body is just trying to keep you safe. But tools, such as grounding exercises and mindfulness, can help calm these reactions and bring you back to the present moment.

Words like self-compassion and resilience remind us that mental health isn't only about challenges; it's also how we treat ourselves and how we bounce back. Self-compassion means being kind to yourself like you would to a friend. Resilience is your ability to recover from tough times. Both are skills you can build over time, and they're just as important as any other technique. The more you understand these terms, the easier it becomes to talk about what you're feeling and take steps toward healing. Remember, you're not alone. Learning the language of mental health is a step toward understanding yourself, communicating with others, and feeling more in control.

FILL EACH DAY WITH

DATE :

BREATHE BEFORE WRITING...

INHALE EXHALE INHALE EXHALE INHALE EXHALE

WHAT ARE 3 GOOD THINGS WHICH HAPPENED TODAY?

WHAT POSITIVITY DID I PUT OUT INTO THE WORLD TODAY?

WHAT IS MY FAVORITE MOMENT OF THE DAY?

> "I can't change the direction of the wind, but I can adjust my sails to always reach my destination."
> - Jimmy Dean

WHAT ARE 3 SMALL THINGS I APPRECIATED TODAY?

WHAT ARE MY WINS FOR TODAY?

DESCRIBE TODAY IN 1 WORD.

WHAT ARE MY GOALS FOR TOMORROW?

Understanding Anxiety: Your Body's Alarm System

Anxiety is your mind and body's way of trying to keep you safe. Think of it like the smoke detector in your house. When it senses danger—real or imagined—it goes off to get your attention. You hear the beeping, and your heart might race, your palms might get sweaty, or your thoughts might start imagining the worst. This is your body's way of saying, "Pay attention!" For example, feeling nervous before a job interview, a big game, or a performance is normal, only some people experience anxiety more frequently or intensely. It's your brain's way of helping you focus and prepare.

In small amounts, anxiety can be helpful. It keeps you alert and ready for challenges. Imagine you're about to cross a busy street—anxiety reminds you to look both ways, so you don't get hurt. But sometimes, that smoke detector gets stuck in the "on" position. It goes off nonstop even when there's no smoke. Instead of helping you, it makes it harder to think, relax, or enjoy what's happening around you.

When anxiety starts to feel overwhelming or never-ending, remember it's a common experience and there's nothing wrong with you. It just means your brain and body are working too hard to keep you safe. You might feel worried about things that haven't happened yet or that you're carrying a heavy burden. But here's the good news: just like any smoke detector, anxiety can be managed and quieted with the right tools and support.

Many strategies are available to help calm that smoke detector. Simple things such as deep breathing, focusing on the present moment, or talking to a person you trust can make a big difference. You're not alone in feeling this way. Anxiety is a normal human experience, so it's okay to ask for help when you need it. With time and practice, you can learn to manage it and find calm in your mind and body. You're doing your best, and that's more than enough.

Additional Thoughts & Reflection

FILL EACH DAY WITH

DATE :

BREATHE BEFORE WRITING...

INHALE
EXHALE
INHALE
EXHALE
INHALE
EXHALE

WHAT ARE 3 GOOD THINGS WHICH HAPPENED TODAY?

WHAT POSITIVITY DID I PUT OUT INTO THE WORLD TODAY?

WHAT IS MY FAVORITE MOMENT OF THE DAY?

> "Believe in your dreams and they may come true;
> believe in yourself and they will come true."
> - Unknown

WHAT ARE 3 SMALL THINGS I APPRECIATED TODAY?

WHAT ARE MY WINS FOR TODAY?

DESCRIBE TODAY IN 1 WORD.

WHAT ARE MY GOALS FOR TOMORROW?

Common Causes of Anxiety

Anxiety often has underlying causes that can be understood and managed. Understanding the reasons behind why we feel anxious can help us manage our anxiety better. Sometimes, it's rooted within our genetics and brain chemistry. If your parents or other relatives have struggled with anxiety, you might be more likely to as well. It also has to do with how the brain regulates mood and stress. When chemicals such as serotonin, norepinephrine, and dopamine are out of balance, it can make us feel more anxious. Hormonal changes during big life moments, especially puberty, pregnancy, or menopause, can also increase those anxious feelings a hundredfold.

Other times, anxiety is triggered by what's happening around us. Experiencing or witnessing something traumatic—like an accident or violence—can leave emotional scars, making it hard to feel calm. Positive or negative life changes can also create stress. Work can play a huge role, whether it's working too much, dealing with tough coworkers, or feeling overwhelmed. Family responsibilities, expectations, finances, or caregiving duties can also make it hard to relax and increase stress levels.

The way we think often adds fuel to the anxiety fire. Negative self-talk, like saying, "I'll never be good enough," can increase your anxiety. Perfectionism—trying to meet impossible standards—can make you feel like you're falling short. These thought patterns turn small challenges into overwhelming obstacles.

Our daily habits also contribute to worsening anxiety. Poor nutrition, lack of sleep, or not drinking enough water throws your body off balance. Too much caffeine (from coffee or energy drinks) overstimulates your system, causing your heart to race that mimics symptoms of anxiety. Substance use, like alcohol or certain drugs, interferes with your brain's ability to stay balanced. Triggers—specific experiences—can set off your anxiety. Some are obvious, such as public speaking; others are more subtle, like a song or smell that reminds you of something negative. Learning your triggers helps build awareness so you can manage anxiety.

Anxiety is a complex and individual experience; each person faces their own issues and requires different strategies for managing it. It's not about blaming yourself for feeling this way—it's about recognizing the different pieces that come together to make up your experience. When you understand where your anxiety comes from, it becomes easier to find ways to manage it and take back control. You're not alone in this, and there are tools and support to help you treat it.

I've organized this information into a quick reference table for you.

Biological	Environmental	Thought Patterns	Lifestyle
Genetics	Trauma	Negative Self-Talk	Lack of Sleep
Brain Chemistry	Life Transitions	Perfectionism	Poor Diet
Hormones	Work Stress	Catastrophizing	Overuse of Stimulants
	Family Pressure		Substance Use

FILL EACH DAY WITH

DATE :

BREATHE BEFORE WRITING...

INHALE EXHALE INHALE EXHALE INHALE EXHALE

WHAT ARE 3 GOOD THINGS WHICH HAPPENED TODAY?

WHAT POSITIVITY DID I PUT OUT INTO THE WORLD TODAY?

WHAT IS MY FAVORITE MOMENT OF THE DAY?

> "You miss 100% of the shots you don't take."
> - Wayne Gretzky

WHAT ARE 3 SMALL THINGS I APPRECIATED TODAY?

WHAT ARE MY WINS FOR TODAY?

DESCRIBE TODAY IN 1 WORD.

WHAT ARE MY GOALS FOR TOMORROW?

How Thoughts, Emotions, and Behaviors Are Connected

Did you know that your thoughts, feelings, and actions are like three best friends who always hang out together? They're connected in what's called the CBT triangle: Thoughts   Emotions   Behaviors. When one of them changes, it affects the other two. For example, let's say you're thinking, "I'm going to fail at this performance." That thought makes you feel anxious or scared. When you feel that way, you might decide to avoid practicing or even skip the performance entirely. And the end result? That behavior makes the fear grow even bigger. It's all connected.

Sometimes, the way we think can make anxiety worse. These thought patterns are called cognitive distortions and trick us into seeing things in a way that aren't true. Let's look at a few examples:

- Catastrophizing is when your mind jumps to the worst-case scenario, such as thinking, "If I make one mistake, I'll lose my job."
- Black-and-white thinking is when you only see things in extremes, like "I have to be perfect, or I'm a total failure." There are no shades of gray that allow you to make mistakes or learn something new.
- Mind-reading happens when you assume others are judging you, even though you don't have proof, such as, "They must think I'm terrible at this."

These distortions aren't your fault; they're just habits your brain has learned over time. The good news is, you can challenge these thought patterns and teach your brain new habits. This is called cognitive restructuring, and it's like being a detective for your mind. Here's how it works:

- Step 1: Identify the thought. What's the anxious thought running through your mind? Write it down.
- Step 2: Examine the evidence. Ask yourself, "Where's the proof this thought is true? Where's the proof that it's not?" You might realize you're missing important

facts.
- Step 3: Replace the thought. Swap out the anxious thought with one that's more neutral or supportive in nature. For example, instead of thinking, "I'm going to fail," try, "I might not be perfect, but I can do my best, and that's enough."

Here's something you can try right now:
- Think of a recent time when you felt anxious. What thought popped into your head? Write it down.
- Then, ask yourself what evidence supports that thought and what evidence contradicts it.
- Finally, come up with a different way to look at the situation.

It takes practice, but over time, you'll start to notice that your thoughts don't control you. In fact, you have the power to change them. And when you change your thoughts, your feelings and actions start to shift too. It's all connected!

FILL EACH DAY WITH

DATE :

BREATHE BEFORE WRITING...

INHALE EXHALE INHALE EXHALE INHALE EXHALE

WHAT ARE 3 GOOD THINGS WHICH HAPPENED TODAY?

WHAT POSITIVITY DID I PUT OUT INTO THE WORLD TODAY?

WHAT IS MY FAVORITE MOMENT OF THE DAY?

> "The only person you are destined to become is the person you decide to be."
> - Ralph Waldo Emerson

WHAT ARE 3 SMALL THINGS I APPRECIATED TODAY?

WHAT ARE MY WINS FOR TODAY?

DESCRIBE TODAY IN 1 WORD.

WHAT ARE MY GOALS FOR TOMORROW?

Positivity and Its Impact on Mental Health

Positivity is about where you choose to focus your thoughts. It doesn't mean ignoring the tough stuff or pretending everything is perfect. It's about finding a balance—acknowledging the hard parts of life while also looking for what's good, what's working, and what gives you hope. Instead of getting stuck in the "what ifs" or problems, positivity helps you shift toward solutions and strengths. It's like being caught in the rain and finding the joy to dance in it or spotting a rainbow forming in the sky.

Let's be clear—positivity isn't about forcing yourself to be happy all the time or ignoring your feelings. That's called "toxic positivity," and it's not helpful. Positivity means making space for your emotions, even the tough ones, while still believing things can get better. Say to yourself: "What's one small step I can take to feel a tiny bit better?"

The science behind positivity is fascinating. Did you know that positive thinking can rewire your brain to enhance your mood and outlook? Your brain has something called neuroplasticity, which means it can adapt and form new connections over time. When you focus on positive thoughts or practice gratitude, your brain starts releases serotonin and dopamine; these feel-good chemicals help you feel calm, happy, and motivated. Over time, positive thinking increases your brain's ability to be wired for calmness and hope.

Beyond mental well-being, positivity extends its benefits to your physical health as well. When you focus on the good, your body produces less cortisol, which is the stress hormone that leaves you feeling anxious and drained. Lower cortisol levels offer better sleep, a stronger immune system, and generally improved physical health. Positivity can also strengthen your relationships with people by helping you build resilience and connect more deeply with others. When you're feeling good, it's easier to show kindness, patience, and love to those around you.

So, how can you bring more positivity into your life? Start small. Write down three things you're grateful for every day, whether it's the warmth of a morning coffee, a supportive friend, or a moment of peace in your busy day. Practice saying affirmations like, "I can handle this," or "I'm doing my best, and that's enough."

Spend time with people who uplift you and remind you of your strengths. Positivity isn't about ignoring the hard stuff, rather, it's about making space for the good while you work through the tough. And the best part? It does get easier if you keep practicing it.

FILL EACH DAY WITH

DATE :

BREATHE BEFORE WRITING...

INHALE EXHALE INHALE EXHALE INHALE EXHALE

WHAT ARE 3 GOOD THINGS WHICH HAPPENED TODAY?

WHAT POSITIVITY DID I PUT OUT INTO THE WORLD TODAY?

WHAT IS MY FAVORITE MOMENT OF THE DAY?

> "Believe in yourself, take on your challenges, dig deep within yourself to conquer fears. Never let anyone bring you down. You got this."
> - Chantal Sutherland

WHAT ARE 3 SMALL THINGS I APPRECIATED TODAY?

WHAT ARE MY WINS FOR TODAY?

DESCRIBE TODAY IN 1 WORD.

WHAT ARE MY GOALS FOR TOMORROW?

Time to Add the Water

Week 1: Positive Experiences

Write briefly about the times when you displayed each
of the following qualities

Courage	
Kindness	
Selflessness	
Love	
Excitement	
Creativy	
Happiness	
Calm	

Additional Thoughts & Reflection

_____
_____
_____
_____
_____
_____
_____
_____
_____
_____
_____
_____
_____
_____
_____
_____
_____
_____
_____
_____
_____
_____

Additional Thoughts & Reflection

Additional Thoughts & Reflection

Week 2:
Mindfulness and Grounding Techniques
To Build Coping Strategies

FILL EACH DAY WITH

DATE :

BREATHE BEFORE WRITING...

INHALE EXHALE INHALE EXHALE INHALE EXHALE

WHAT ARE 3 GOOD THINGS WHICH HAPPENED TODAY?

WHAT POSITIVITY DID I PUT OUT INTO THE WORLD TODAY?

WHAT IS MY FAVORITE MOMENT OF THE DAY?

> *"The only time you should ever look back is to see how far you've come."*
> *- Unknown*

WHAT ARE 3 SMALL THINGS I APPRECIATED TODAY?

WHAT ARE MY WINS FOR TODAY?

DESCRIBE TODAY IN 1 WORD.

WHAT ARE MY GOALS FOR TOMORROW?

The Role of Mindfulness in Reducing Anxiety

Mindfulness is like pressing the pause button when your thoughts are spinning out of control. At its core, mindfulness is being fully present in the moment and paying attention to what's happening without judgment. It's noticing your thoughts, emotions, and feelings in your body without labeling them as good or bad. This is especially helpful when anxiety tries to pull you into endless "what if" scenarios regarding events that haven't happened. Mindfulness gently brings you back to what's real and happening now.

When you feel anxious, your brain's alarm system, the amygdala, goes into overdrive. When the amygdala is active, it's as if your body is yelling "Danger!" even when there's nothing threatening you. Mindfulness acts like a calming voice, reminding you that you're safe. Studies show mindfulness reduces activity in the amygdala, which can reduce the fight-or-flight response, which makes anxiety feel so intense. At the same time, mindfulness strengthens your prefrontal cortex—the part of your brain helping you focus, make decisions, and stay in control. This means mindfulness doesn't just help in the moment; it can help your brain work better over time.

There are a lot of ways to practice mindfulness that go beyond deep breathing. Grounding exercises are a great place to start because they help you connect with the world immediately around you and pull your focus away from anxious thoughts. One popular method is the 5-4-3-2-1 technique. Look around and name five things you can see, four things you can touch, three things you can hear, two things you can smell, and one thing you can taste. This short exercise reminds your brain you're in the present, allowing you to quiet those racing thoughts.

Another grounding technique is holding an object. Grab something nearby, such as a smooth rock, a soft blanket, or a cup of tea. Focus on its texture, temperature, and weight. This connection to touch brings your attention to something real and tangible. You can also try visual grounding, where you pick one thing to focus on, such as a painting, a tree outside, or the details of a favorite object, and spend a minute observing it closely. Notice the colors, shapes, and patterns—it's like giving your mind a little break from worrying.

Movement grounding is another powerful tool. Stand up and press your feet firmly into the ground. Wiggle your toes, rock back and forth, and feel how your body connects to the floor beneath you. This simple movement can help you feel more anchored. Similarly, naming categories is a way to focus your mind. For example, name as many animals, colors, or favorite foods as you can. This distracts your brain from spiraling thoughts and brings it back to something neutral and manageable.

Engaging your senses is also key. Light a scented candle or use essential oils to focus on a calming smell, or listen to soothing music and pay attention to the different instruments or lyrics. Even physical grounding, such as walking barefoot on grass, hugging yourself, or taking a warm shower, can remind your body that you're safe and supported. These exercises may seem small, but they create moments of calm that build up over time.

Mindfulness takes practice, and it's okay if it feels strange or awkward at first. Start small, with just a few minutes each day, whether that's using one of these grounding exercises, journaling your thoughts, or simply noticing the sounds and colors around you. With time, these practices will feel more natural, and you'll find they quiet your anxious mind and bring you back to a place of peace. You're not alone, and every small step you take is progress. You've got this!

FILL EACH DAY WITH

DATE :

BREATHE BEFORE WRITING...

INHALE EXHALE INHALE EXHALE INHALE EXHALE

WHAT ARE 3 GOOD THINGS WHICH HAPPENED TODAY?

WHAT POSITIVITY DID I PUT OUT INTO THE WORLD TODAY?

WHAT IS MY FAVORITE MOMENT OF THE DAY?

> "Believe in the power of your dreams and the universe will work with you to make them come true."
> - Unknown

WHAT ARE 3 SMALL THINGS I APPRECIATED TODAY?

WHAT ARE MY WINS FOR TODAY?

DESCRIBE TODAY IN 1 WORD.

WHAT ARE MY GOALS FOR TOMORROW?

Additional Thoughts & Reflection

Additional Thoughts & Reflection

_____

_____

_____

_____

_____

_____

_____

_____

_____

_____

_____

_____

_____

_____

_____

_____

_____

_____

_____

_____

_____

_____

FILL EACH DAY WITH

DATE :

BREATHE BEFORE WRITING...

INHALE EXHALE INHALE EXHALE INHALE EXHALE

WHAT ARE 3 GOOD THINGS WHICH HAPPENED TODAY?

WHAT POSITIVITY DID I PUT OUT INTO THE WORLD TODAY?

WHAT IS MY FAVORITE MOMENT OF THE DAY?

> "Happiness is not something ready-made. It comes from your own actions."
> - Dalai Lama

WHAT ARE 3 SMALL THINGS I APPRECIATED TODAY?

WHAT ARE MY WINS FOR TODAY?

DESCRIBE TODAY IN 1 WORD.

WHAT ARE MY GOALS FOR TOMORROW?

Using Your Senses to Feel Calm

When you feel worried or scared, your body and mind can feel out of control. But did you know that your senses are capable of helping you feel better? They can help bring you back to the present. It's a great way to calm down when anxiety tries to take over.

Sight
Looking at things around you can help you feel safe. Find five things you can see right now. Maybe you notice a tree outside, a favorite toy, or a soft pillow. Colors, shapes, and lights help your mind slow down. Take a few moments to describe something you see in detail. If you feel anxious, look at something that makes you happy, such as a picture of someone you love or a beautiful sunset.

Hearing
Listening to sounds can help you feel calm. Close your eyes and listen to what is around you. Can you hear birds singing, music playing, or the sound of the wind? Soft and gentle sounds, like ocean waves or quiet music, aids in your body relaxing. Hum your favorite song or listen to calming sounds when you feel nervous.

Touch
Touching things can make you feel safe and grounded. Hold something soft, like a fuzzy blanket or a stuffed animal, or run your fingers over something smooth or rough to focus on how it feels. Try eating something and focusing on the texture of the food in your mouth. Some people like squeezing a stress ball or rubbing their hands together. The feeling of touch reminds your body that you are safe and in the present.

Smell
Scents can change how you feel. Take a deep breath in, and notice what you smell. Maybe it's fresh air, yummy food, or a flower nearby. Set up several scents, close your eyes, and guess which scent you are smelling. When you smell something nice, like a scented candle or a favorite lotion, it can help your body feel more relaxed. If you feel anxious, try smelling something that reminds you of a happy time.

Taste

Eating or drinking something can also help you feel calm. Take small bites of something tasty, like a piece of fruit or a mint. Notice how it feels in your mouth. Drinking a warm cup of tea or cold water can also help your body feel safe. Focusing on taste helps your mind slow down and enjoy the present.

Bringing It All Together

Whenever you feel anxious, try using your senses to feel better. Look around, listen to calming sounds, touch something comforting, smell something nice, or taste something soothing. Your senses can remind you that you're not in harm's way and help you feel at ease. The more you practice, the easier it will be to use your senses to manage anxiety.

FILL EACH DAY WITH

DATE :

BREATHE BEFORE WRITING...

INHALE EXHALE INHALE EXHALE INHALE EXHALE

WHAT ARE 3 GOOD THINGS WHICH HAPPENED TODAY?

WHAT POSITIVITY DID I PUT OUT INTO THE WORLD TODAY?

WHAT IS MY FAVORITE MOMENT OF THE DAY?

> "It does not matter how slowly you go as long as you do not stop."
> - Confucius

WHAT ARE 3 SMALL THINGS I APPRECIATED TODAY?

WHAT ARE MY WINS FOR TODAY?

DESCRIBE TODAY IN 1 WORD.

WHAT ARE MY GOALS FOR TOMORROW?

A Mindful Moment
Body Scan

If you would like to listen to this exercise, please scan the QR code at the end of the book to access your online course companion. The course companion includes a recorded version of this exercise.

Take a few moments to settle into a comfortable position—whether you're sitting back in a chair or lying down. If you're okay with it, gently close your eyes or let your gaze soften. Now, take a deep breath in ... and let it out slowly.

Over the next few minutes, we're going to tune into your body. You might notice the feeling of your clothes on your skin, the tension in your muscles, the temperature of the air around you, or maybe nothing at all. And that's perfectly okay. Your only job is to notice—there's no need to change anything or do anything differently. Just observe.

Let's start at your feet. Notice how they feel—your soles, your heels, your toes, and the tops of your feet. Can you feel the ground beneath you? Maybe the texture of your shoes or socks? Take a moment to check in with what's happening there.

Now, move your attention to your ankles, shins, and calves. What do you feel in those muscles? Are they tense? Relaxed? Notice the deeper sensations in your muscles and the surface of your skin.

Next, shift your focus to your knees and thighs. Can you feel your clothes brushing against your skin? Observe whatever comes up, without judgment.

Let's move on to your hips and lower back. How do they feel right now? Maybe there's pressure from the surface you're sitting or lying on. Just notice it, no need to do anything else.

Take a few moments to tune into your breathing. Feel your belly rise as you inhale ... and fall as you exhale. Let each breath flow naturally.

Now, notice the sensations in your upper back and chest. Maybe you can feel your shirt against your skin or the air moving as you breathe.

Turn your attention to your hands, fingers, and wrists. What do you notice there? Any warmth, tingling, or pressure?

Move up to your forearms, upper arms, and shoulders. Observe the feelings—whether it's tension, relaxation, or anything in between.

Now, check in with your neck and throat. Do you notice any tightness or softness? Acknowledge whatever is present.

Finally, let your awareness settle on your face and head. Pay attention to each part—your forehead, eyes, cheeks, and jaw. Notice how everything feels in this moment.

Before we wrap up, let's take one last slow scan of your whole body—from your toes to the top of your head. Notice anything that stands out, or simply recognize the sense of being present.

And now, when you're ready, slowly open your eyes, bringing yourself back to the space around you.

FILL EACH DAY WITH

DATE :

Positivity

BREATHE BEFORE WRITING...

INHALE EXHALE INHALE EXHALE INHALE EXHALE

WHAT ARE 3 GOOD THINGS WHICH HAPPENED TODAY?

WHAT POSITIVITY DID I PUT OUT INTO THE WORLD TODAY?

WHAT IS MY FAVORITE MOMENT OF THE DAY?

> "When you focus on problems, you'll have more problems. When you focus on possibilities, you'll have more opportunities."
> - Unknown

WHAT ARE 3 SMALL THINGS I APPRECIATED TODAY?

WHAT ARE MY WINS FOR TODAY?

DESCRIBE TODAY IN 1 WORD.

WHAT ARE MY GOALS FOR TOMORROW?

A Mindful Moment Breathwork

If you would like to listen to this exercise, please scan the QR code at the end of the book to access your online course companion. The course companion includes a recorded version of this exercise.

Let's get started by finding a position that's comfortable for you—one where you won't doze off. You can sit cross-legged on the floor, in a chair with your feet flat on the ground, or whatever feels natural. Just make sure you're in a position where you can stay alert yet relaxed.

If it feels right, go ahead and close your eyes or pick a soft spot in the room to focus on. Let your shoulders roll forward slowly, then back. Lean your head gently from side to side—left ear toward your left shoulder, then right ear toward your right shoulder. Release any tension you feel creeping up, knowing your body will continue to relax as you settle into this meditation.

Now, let's focus on your breath. Notice how it flows in and out, without trying to change or control it. Let your body breathe the way it naturally knows how. Take a moment to tune in and simply observe.

Picture your breath moving in and out of your body, like a gentle wave. If your mind starts to wander (and trust me, it will—that's normal), bring your attention back to the flow of your breathing. No judgment, just awareness. Any stray thoughts can come and go without pulling you away from the rhythm of your breath.

Now, really notice each breath—how it starts with an inhale, the slight pause, the exhale, and the tiny pause before the next breath. There's no rush here. Your breath is steady and calm, flowing naturally.

Feel the air as it enters through your nose, moving through your body. Imagine it flowing down into your lungs, filling the space gently. And as you exhale, notice how that space slowly gets smaller. Let your chest and stomach rise and fall in a relaxed, easy way.

Let's start counting our breaths now. As you breathe in, silently count "one." As you exhale, count "one" again. Keep going like this—inhale, "one"… exhale, "one." The idea is to keep it simple, without any pressure to get it perfect.

Notice how your body feels now—calm, grounded, and relaxed. Your breathing is gentle, and your mind is starting to feel more at ease.

When you're ready, let's gently reawaken. Keep your eyes closed for now and start to notice the sounds around you. Feel the surface beneath you and the sensation of your clothes on your skin. Wiggle your fingers and toes; give your shoulders a little shrug.

When you're ready, open your eyes. But don't rush—stay sitting for a moment, soaking in that sense of relaxation. Stretch your arms and legs, ease yourself back to the present, and when you're ready, slowly stand up.

As you move through the rest of your day, notice how this practice has given you a little more energy and a lot more calm.

FILL EACH DAY WITH

DATE :

Positivity

BREATHE BEFORE WRITING...

INHALE EXHALE INHALE EXHALE INHALE EXHALE

WHAT ARE 3 GOOD THINGS WHICH HAPPENED TODAY?

WHAT POSITIVITY DID I PUT OUT INTO THE WORLD TODAY?

WHAT IS MY FAVORITE MOMENT OF THE DAY?

> "When one door of happiness closes, another opens; but often we look so long at the closed door that we do not see the one which has been opened for us."
> - Helen Keller

WHAT ARE 3 SMALL THINGS I APPRECIATED TODAY?

WHAT ARE MY WINS FOR TODAY?

DESCRIBE TODAY IN 1 WORD.

WHAT ARE MY GOALS FOR TOMORROW?

A Mindful Moment Progressive Muscle Relaxation

If you would like to listen to this exercise, please scan the QR code at the end of the book to access your online course companion. The course companion includes a recorded version of this exercise.

Let's start by finding a comfortable spot, either sitting or lying down, somewhere you won't be disturbed for a little while. This is your time to unwind.

Bring your attention fully to your body. If your mind starts to drift (and it probably will), that's okay—just gently guide it back to the muscle group we're focusing on.

Take a deep breath in, filling your lungs completely, and hold it for a moment. Then, let the breath out slowly. Do that again, paying attention to the rise and fall of your stomach. As you exhale, imagine all the tension in your body flowing out with your breath. With each breath, feel your body getting a little more relaxed.

Let's begin. Start by tightening the muscles in your forehead—raise your eyebrows as high as you can. Hold that tension for about five seconds, then let go and feel that stress fall away.

Now, smile as wide as you can, feeling the tension in your mouth and cheeks. Hold it for about five seconds, and release, noticing the softness return to your face.

Next, squint your eyes tightly shut. Hold it for five seconds, and release. Feel the relief as your eyes relax.

Gently tilt your head back, as if you're looking up at the ceiling. Hold that stretch for five seconds, and then let go, feeling the tension melt away as your head and neck relax.

Take a deep breath in … and out. Keep your breathing slow and steady.

Now, clench your fists tightly, but not so much that it strains. Hold for five seconds … and release. Let your fingers relax completely.

Let's move to your arms—flex your biceps, noticing the tension build up. Visualize the muscle tightening, then hold for five seconds … and release. Feel that wave of relaxation flowing in.

Now extend your arms and lock your elbows to tighten your triceps. Hold for five seconds, and release.

Lift your shoulders up like you're trying to touch your ears. Hold for five seconds … and drop them, feeling their weight settle down.

Pull your shoulders back, as if you're trying to make your shoulder blades touch. Hold for five seconds, and release. Feel your upper back ease up.

Take a deep breath into your chest, expanding as much as you can. Hold it for five seconds, and then exhale, blowing away any remaining tension.

Tighten your stomach by sucking it in. Hold for five seconds … and release. Now gently arch your lower back for a little stretch, hold for five seconds, and relax.

Feel your upper body getting looser with every breath.

Now, squeeze your glutes—tighten your buttocks and hold for five seconds. Release, letting your hips relax into the surface below you.

Press your knees together like you're holding a penny between them. Hold for five seconds, and release, feeling the tension let go.

Flex your feet, pulling your toes back toward you to feel the stretch in your calves. Hold it for five seconds, and relax, feeling the weight of your legs sink into the ground.

Finally, curl your toes under to tense up your feet. Hold for five seconds … and release.

Now, take a moment to imagine a wave of relaxation slowly spreading from the top of your head, all the way down to your toes. Feel the weight of your body as it relaxes deeper with each breath.

Breathe in … and out … in … and out. Let yourself enjoy this moment of calm.

FILL EACH DAY WITH

DATE :

BREATHE BEFORE WRITING...

INHALE EXHALE INHALE EXHALE INHALE EXHALE

WHAT ARE 3 GOOD THINGS WHICH HAPPENED TODAY?

WHAT POSITIVITY DID I PUT OUT INTO THE WORLD TODAY?

WHAT IS MY FAVORITE MOMENT OF THE DAY?

> "It does not matter how slowly you go as long as you do not stop."
> - Confucius

WHAT ARE 3 SMALL THINGS I APPRECIATED TODAY?

WHAT ARE MY WINS FOR TODAY?

DESCRIBE TODAY IN 1 WORD.

WHAT ARE MY GOALS FOR TOMORROW?

A Mindful Moment
Mindful Listening

*If you would like to listen to this exercise, please scan the QR code at the end of the book to access your online course companion. The course companion includes a recorded version of this exercise.**

This script is best if read by one person to the person meditating. A wind chime, bell or other gentle sounding instrument would be useful for this session.

Settling In
Let's begin by getting comfortable. Find a position where you can relax and settle in—whether you're sitting or lying down, just make sure you feel supported. Give your body a little wiggle to release any tension, then let yourself settle into stillness.

Mindful meditation is about being present. There's no right way to do this—it's not about having a specific experience or doing it perfectly. Just focus on what's happening right now, and let your mind settle as best as it can.

Main Practice
Let's start by tuning in to your breath. Where do you feel it the most in your body? Maybe it's in your stomach, your chest, or even at your nose or mouth. Wherever it is, notice the sensations that come with each breath.

As you breathe in and out, ask yourself: How does my breath feel? There's no need to change anything—just observe.

Now, shift your focus to your sense of hearing. Listen to the sound of your breath. It's not about making it louder or heavier; notice it as it is. Keep breathing normally, but really tune in to the sound.

Next, let's expand your awareness to the other sounds around you. Maybe it's a ticking clock, the hum of the air, or sounds from outside the room. Whatever it is, just listen. If your mind wanders (which it probably will), that's okay. Simply notice it and gently bring your focus back to what you hear.

Now, let's take it a step further. We're going to focus on a particular sound—a bell, a wind chime, or whatever gentle sound we're using today. Keep your eyes closed and listen carefully. What comes to mind when you hear it? Are there any words, images, or feelings that arise? Notice whatever thoughts or memories the sound brings up.

Now, listen for the sound again. This time, I'll move to a different part of the room before making the sound. Has anything changed? Does the sound seem to come from a different direction? Pay close attention to where the sound is coming from.

I'll move again, and each time you hear the sound, just focus on it, noticing any shifts or changes. Let's repeat this a few times, letting your focus rest entirely on the sound.

Now, let's add one more layer of mindfulness. Each time you hear the sound, bring your attention to a different part of your body. Start with your feet, then work your way up—your legs, your torso, your arms, and so on. Notice any sensations in that area as you listen to the sound. Let's repeat this a few times, tuning into both the sound and your body.

Take a deep breath and release it noticing how you feel in the moment. Take another and release it along with any negativity you've noticed yourself experiencing. Take a final deep breath, in and out, and you are ready to return to your day.

Time to Add the Lemons

Week 2: Reminder to Myself

I like the fact that I ...

My skills and strengths are ...

I love being myself when ...

The best event in my life was when ...

Additional Thoughts & Reflection

_____
_____
_____
_____
_____
_____
_____
_____
_____
_____
_____
_____
_____
_____
_____
_____
_____
_____
_____
_____
_____
_____

Additional Thoughts & Reflection

Additional Thoughts & Reflection

Week 3:
Managing Anxiety with Actionable Techniques
AKA Learning Practical Tools

FILL EACH DAY WITH

DATE :

BREATHE BEFORE WRITING...

INHALE EXHALE INHALE EXHALE INHALE EXHALE

WHAT ARE 3 GOOD THINGS WHICH HAPPENED TODAY?

WHAT POSITIVITY DID I PUT OUT INTO THE WORLD TODAY?

WHAT IS MY FAVORITE MOMENT OF THE DAY?

> "Believe you can and you're halfway there."
> - Theodore Roosevelt

WHAT ARE 3 SMALL THINGS I APPRECIATED TODAY?

WHAT ARE MY WINS FOR TODAY?

DESCRIBE TODAY IN 1 WORD.

WHAT ARE MY GOALS FOR TOMORROW?

Techniques to Manage Anxiety

When anxiety shows up, it can feel like it's taking over everything, but there are ways to regain a sense of control. Techniques and mindfulness-based grounding exercises can help address it, but there are differences between them. Techniques are specific actions or tools you use to shift your focus, calm your mind, or reset your body. These steps help you tackle anxiety directly, while grounding exercises help you stay connected to the present. Let's explore a few techniques you can try.

One effective technique is visualization. This involves closing your eyes and imagining a peaceful place, such as a beach, your bed, or a favorite memory. Picture every detail—the sounds, the smells, the colors—use all your senses and let yourself feel like you're really there. Visualization works by giving your brain a break from the anxious thoughts by replacing them with calming or positive images.

Another helpful technique is self-talk rephrasing. When anxiety makes you think negative things such as, "I can't do this," challenge it by saying, "I can try my best, and that's enough." Or if you're thinking, "Something bad will happen," try saying, "I don't know what will happen, but I'll handle it if it does." This practice helps you reframe anxious thoughts into something neutral, manageable, and less scary.

Scripting is another technique you can use to prepare for anxious situations. Write down a conversation or scenario that makes you nervous; include responses you can use to stay calm. For example, if you're worried about a difficult conversation, write down what you'd like to say and practice it. This helps you feel prepared and reduces anxiety about the unknown.

Physical techniques like movement breaks are also effective. If you feel anxious, get up and move around. Stretch your arms high, do a few squats, or shake out your hands. Moving releases tension in your body and clears your mind. Five minutes of gentle movement can make a huge difference or go big by doing five minutes of dancing.

Last, journaling can help untangle your thoughts. Write down whatever's on your mind, no matter how big or small. Seeing your worries on paper helps you process them and often makes them feel less overwhelming. Pair this with writing one solution or positive thought for each worry to help shift your focus.

These techniques may feel uncomfortable at first, and that's okay. The more you practice, the easier it becomes to find what works best for you. Remember, techniques are like tools in a toolbox—you don't have to use them all. Pick one that feels right in the moment and trust every baby step will help. Whether you're visualizing, reframing your thoughts, or moving your body, you're managing your anxiety, one step at a time. You've got this!

FILL EACH DAY WITH

DATE :

BREATHE BEFORE WRITING...

INHALE EXHALE INHALE EXHALE INHALE EXHALE

WHAT ARE 3 GOOD THINGS WHICH HAPPENED TODAY?

WHAT POSITIVITY DID I PUT OUT INTO THE WORLD TODAY?

WHAT IS MY FAVORITE MOMENT OF THE DAY?

> "Every day may not be good, but there is something good in every day."
> - Unknown

WHAT ARE 3 SMALL THINGS I APPRECIATED TODAY?

WHAT ARE MY WINS FOR TODAY?

DESCRIBE TODAY IN 1 WORD.

WHAT ARE MY GOALS FOR TOMORROW?

Additional Thoughts & Reflection

Additional Thoughts & Reflection

_____
_____
_____
_____
_____
_____
_____
_____
_____
_____
_____
_____
_____
_____
_____
_____
_____
_____
_____
_____
_____
_____
_____

FILL EACH DAY WITH

DATE :

BREATHE BEFORE WRITING...

INHALE   EXHALE   INHALE   EXHALE   INHALE   EXHALE

WHAT ARE 3 GOOD THINGS WHICH HAPPENED TODAY?

WHAT POSITIVITY DID I PUT OUT INTO THE WORLD TODAY?

WHAT IS MY FAVORITE MOMENT OF THE DAY?

> "I have not failed. I've just found 10,000 ways that won't work."
> - Thomas Edison

WHAT ARE 3 SMALL THINGS I APPRECIATED TODAY?

WHAT ARE MY WINS FOR TODAY?

DESCRIBE TODAY IN 1 WORD.

WHAT ARE MY GOALS FOR TOMORROW?

A Mindful Moment
Reframing Negative
Thoughts

*If you would like to listen to this exercise, please scan the QR code at the end of the book to access your online course companion. The course companion includes a recorded version of this exercise.***

Reframing negative thoughts into positive ones is a great way to improve your mood, build resilience, and enhance your overall well-being. Here are seven steps you can take to reframe negative thoughts into positive ones:

- Spot the negative thought: Start by noticing that negative thought swirling around in your mind. It might be self-doubt, worry, or a negative interpretation of a situation. Whatever it is, simply acknowledge it. That awareness is your first step.

- Challenge the negative thought: Now that you've identified the thought, ask yourself—does this thought really hold up? Is it the absolute truth, or is there another way to look at the situation? This step helps you step back and see things a little more objectively, reducing the impact of negative emotions associated with the thought.

- Reframe the negative thought: Once you have challenged the negative thought, it's time to reframe it. Try finding a more positive or neutral way to put it. For example, instead of thinking, "I'll never be able to do this," try shifting it to, "This is tough, but I've got the skills and resources to figure it out." It's all about changing the narrative.

- Practice gratitude: Incorporating gratitude into your day can help you reframe negative thoughts. When you focus on what's going right, the negatives seem less overwhelming and you are less likely to get bogged down by negative thoughts and emotions. Make a habit of noticing what you're grateful for—even the small stuff—because it shifts your perspective and boosts your overall outlook.

- Practice mindfulness: Mindfulness practices, like meditation or just a few deep breaths, can help you stay in the moment. When you're present, those negative

- thoughts lose some of their power. Observing your thoughts without judgment can give you a sense of control, and help you handle emotions as they come.

- Surround yourself with positivity: What you surround yourself with matters. Whether it's positive people, uplifting content, or an environment that inspires you, being in a positive space helps you keep your mindset on track. By immersing yourself in positivity, you are more likely to adopt a positive mindset and reduce the impact of negative thoughts and emotions.

- Make it a habit: Reframing takes practice. The more you do it, the easier it becomes to catch negative thoughts and turn them around. It's not about pretending everything's perfect—it's about training your mind to look for the possibilities, the solutions, and the silver linings.

By following these steps and making an effort to reframe negative thoughts into positive ones, you can create a stronger, more positive mindset.

FILL EACH DAY WITH

DATE :

BREATHE BEFORE WRITING...

INHALE EXHALE INHALE EXHALE INHALE EXHALE

WHAT ARE 3 GOOD THINGS WHICH HAPPENED TODAY?

WHAT POSITIVITY DID I PUT OUT INTO THE WORLD TODAY?

WHAT IS MY FAVORITE MOMENT OF THE DAY?

"Believe in yourself and all that you are. Know that there is something inside you that is greater than any obstacle."
- Christian D. Larson

WHAT ARE 3 SMALL THINGS I APPRECIATED TODAY?

WHAT ARE MY WINS FOR TODAY?

DESCRIBE TODAY IN 1 WORD.

WHAT ARE MY GOALS FOR TOMORROW?

A Mindful Moment
Loving Kindness Meditation

*If you would like to listen to this exercise, please scan the QR code at the end of the book to access your online course companion. The course companion includes a recorded version of this exercise.**

Let's begin by getting into a comfortable position. Whether you're seated or lying down, find a spot where you feel supported and can relax. Place your hands wherever they feel natural—on your lap, on your knees, or by your side.

Now, take a moment to breathe naturally. There's no need to change anything, just notice your breath as it flows in and out.

As we begin, I want you to imagine someone you deeply care about sitting right in front of you. Picture a warm, white light connecting your hearts. Feel that sense of love, affection, and warmth flowing between you.

Take a moment to really connect with those feelings—let them fill your body. Enjoy how it feels to be in this moment, surrounded by love and kindness.

Now, silently say to yourself: "May I be well, happy, and peaceful." Feel that loving-kindness fill every part of you. Then, send those same feelings to your loved one: "May you be well, happy, and peaceful."

As you keep breathing naturally, feel that light connecting you heart-to-heart. Let yourselves be bathed in the warmth and light of loving-kindness. Silently repeat: "May I be well, happy, and peaceful. May you be well, happy, and peaceful."

Keep your breath steady and natural as you feel that light expanding. Now, imagine the white light growing into a circle, wrapping around both you and your loved one, surrounding you with peace and warmth.

Let that light radiate outward, spreading the love and kindness you share to everyone and everything around you—every person, every animal, even the tiniest beings. Feel it reach out into the universe, as far as you can imagine.

Now, silently say: "May we be well, happy, and peaceful. May all beings be well, happy, and peaceful." Keep breathing, keep feeling that connection, and let those words settle in your heart: "May we be well, happy, and peaceful. May all beings be well, happy, and peaceful."

As you sit in this feeling, notice the warmth and expansion in your body. Recognize how this loving-kindness flows from your heart and out into the universe. It's a reflection of the kindness and love that already lives inside you.

Take a moment to tune into your body—notice any feelings and any sensations. Pay attention to what's observing those sensations, that quiet, peaceful part of you that's always present, watching without judgment.

Breathe naturally, and when you're ready, slowly open your eyes.

FILL EACH DAY WITH *Positivity*

DATE :

BREATHE BEFORE WRITING...

INHALE EXHALE INHALE EXHALE INHALE EXHALE

WHAT ARE 3 GOOD THINGS WHICH HAPPENED TODAY?

WHAT POSITIVITY DID I PUT OUT INTO THE WORLD TODAY?

WHAT IS MY FAVORITE MOMENT OF THE DAY?

> "It's not what happens to you that determines how far you will go in life; it is how you handle what happens to you."
> – Zig Ziglar

WHAT ARE 3 SMALL THINGS I APPRECIATED TODAY?

WHAT ARE MY WINS FOR TODAY?

DESCRIBE TODAY IN 1 WORD.

WHAT ARE MY GOALS FOR TOMORROW?

Incorporating Research and Evidence-Based Practices

Did you know there's science behind the tools we use to manage anxiety? You're not just doing random exercises—these are techniques researchers have studied and proven to work. For instance, studies show journaling can reduce anxiety by helping you process your feelings and organize your thoughts. Writing things down allows your brain to let go of some of the clutter, making space for more clarity and bringing calm. It's a simple way to take what's crowding your mind and put it on paper, where it feels a little less overwhelming.

Grounding exercises are also evidence-based techniques great for when anxiety feels like it's overwhelming you. Grounding works by helping you focus on the present instead of the worries in your mind. Grounding exercises reconnects you to your immediate surroundings, reminding you you're safe and in control right now. Research shows grounding exercises can lower your heart rate and reduce the fight-or-flight response.

Gratitude practices are another powerful evidenced-based technique. When you focus on things you're thankful for, your brain releases feel-good chemicals that help you feel happy and calm. Studies have found that regularly practicing gratitude can improve mental health by reducing anxiety and depression. This could be as simple as writing down a few things you're grateful for each day. They don't have to be big—something like a fresh piece of fruit or a kind smile from a stranger can make a difference.

One more evidenced-based technique is cognitive restructuring, which is part of CBT triangle we talked about earlier. Cognitive restructuring helps retrain your brain to think in a way that's a little more helpful and less focused on fear. Over time, this can reduce the intensity of anxious feelings.

Using these research-backed practices isn't about being perfect or doing everything at once. It's about finding small, manageable ways to help yourself feel calmer and in control. These tools have worked for others, and they can work for you too. Remember, it's okay to take things one step at a time. You're doing great just by taking the time to learn!

Additional Thoughts & Reflection

_____
_____
_____
_____
_____
_____
_____
_____
_____
_____
_____
_____
_____
_____
_____
_____
_____
_____
_____
_____
_____
_____
_____

FILL EACH DAY WITH

DATE :

BREATHE BEFORE WRITING...

INHALE EXHALE INHALE EXHALE INHALE EXHALE

WHAT ARE 3 GOOD THINGS WHICH HAPPENED TODAY?

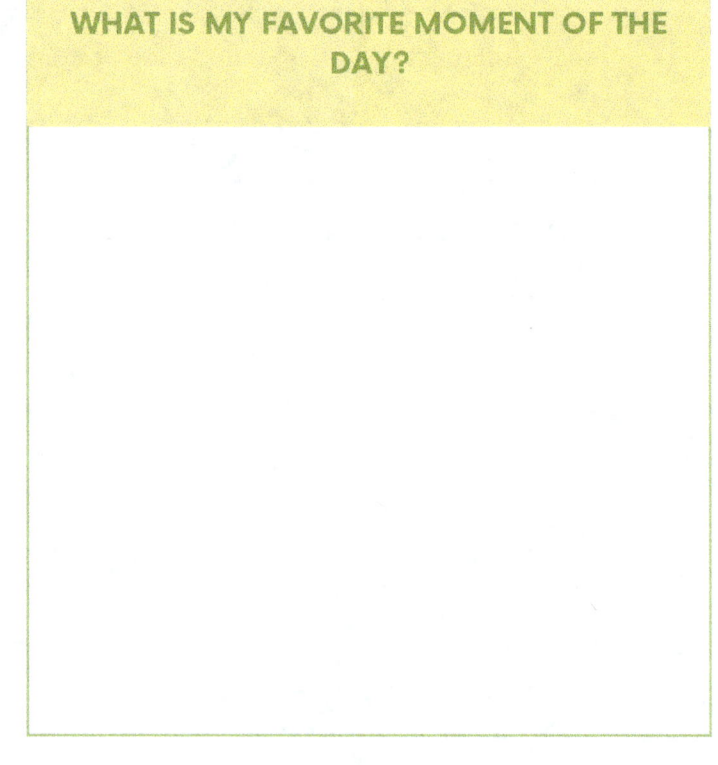

WHAT POSITIVITY DID I PUT OUT INTO THE WORLD TODAY?

WHAT IS MY FAVORITE MOMENT OF THE DAY?

> "Success is not how high you have climbed, but how you make a positive difference to the world."
> - Roy T. Bennett

WHAT ARE 3 SMALL THINGS I APPRECIATED TODAY?

WHAT ARE MY WINS FOR TODAY?

DESCRIBE TODAY IN 1 WORD.

WHAT ARE MY GOALS FOR TOMORROW?

Self Care

Self-care means making time for things that help you live your best life by improving your physical and mental health. When it comes to your mental health, self-care can help you manage stress and lower the risk of illness. Even small actions can have a big impact. Self-care looks different for everyone, and it is important to find what you need and enjoy. It may take time and trial and error to discover what works best for you. It's not a cure-all; it's a supplement to other coping techniques to support your mental health.

On the next page, please identify any barriers that make self-care difficult and any negative coping habits that might've developed as a result. Reflect on your current self-care practice and explore ways to improve it in the following areas:

- Physical: Caring for your body to stay healthy now and in the future.
- Intellectual: Valuing lifelong learning, and responding positively to intellectual challenges.
- Emotional: Understanding and respecting your feelings, values, and attitudes, appreciating the feelings of others and managing your emotions in a constructive way.
- Social: Developing and maintaining healthy relationships and contributing to your community.
- Spiritual: Finding purpose, value, and meaning in your life with or without organized religion and participating in activities that are consistent with your beliefs and values.
- Vocational: Preparing for and participating in work that provides personal satisfaction and life enrichment that is consistent with your values, goals, and lifestyle.
- Financial: Managing your resources to live within your means, making informed financial decisions and investments, setting realistic goals, and preparing for short-term and long-term needs or emergencies.
- Environmental: Understanding how your social, natural, and built environments affect your health and well-being.

- Physical: Caring for your body to stay healthy now and in the future.
- Intellectual: Valuing lifelong learning, and responding positively to intellectual challenges.
- Emotional: Understanding and respecting your feelings, values, and attitudes, appreciating the feelings of others and managing your emotions in a constructive way.
- Social: Developing and maintaining healthy relationships and contributing to your community.
- Spiritual: Finding purpose, value, and meaning in your life with or without organized religion and participating in activities that are consistent with your beliefs and values.
- Vocational: Preparing for and participating in work that provides personal satisfaction and life enrichment that is consistent with your values, goals, and lifestyle.
- Financial: Managing your resources to live within your means, making informed financial decisions and investments, setting realistic goals, and preparing for short-term and long-term needs or emergencies.
- Environmental: Understanding how your social, natural, and built environments affect your health and well-being.

Barriers to Maintaining Self Care	
How I Will Address the Barriers	
Negative Coping Strategies I Currently Use	
Alternative Coping Strategies I Will Try	

My Self Care Plan

Domain	Current Practice	Updated Practice
Physical		
Intellectual		
Emotional		
Social		
Spiritual		
Vocational		
Financial		
Environmental		

Additional Thoughts & Reflection

FILL EACH DAY WITH

DATE :

BREATHE BEFORE WRITING...

INHALE | EXHALE | INHALE | EXHALE | INHALE | EXHALE

WHAT ARE 3 GOOD THINGS WHICH HAPPENED TODAY?

WHAT POSITIVITY DID I PUT OUT INTO THE WORLD TODAY?

WHAT IS MY FAVORITE MOMENT OF THE DAY?

"You have within you right now, everything you need to deal with whatever the world can throw at you."
- Brian Tracy

WHAT ARE 3 SMALL THINGS I APPRECIATED TODAY?

WHAT ARE MY WINS FOR TODAY?

DESCRIBE TODAY IN 1 WORD.

WHAT ARE MY GOALS FOR TOMORROW?

Time to Add the Sugar
Week 3: The *Gratitude* Jar

Write 10 things you are grateful for inside the jar.

THINGS I FEEL GRATEFUL FOR

Additional Thoughts & Reflection

_____
_____
_____
_____
_____
_____
_____
_____
_____
_____
_____
_____
_____
_____
_____
_____
_____
_____
_____
_____
_____
_____

Additional Thoughts & Reflection

Additional Thoughts & Reflection

Week 4:
Reflection and Long-Term Growth

Ways to Build Sustainable Change

FILL EACH DAY WITH

DATE :

BREATHE BEFORE WRITING...

INHALE EXHALE INHALE EXHALE INHALE EXHALE

WHAT ARE 3 GOOD THINGS WHICH HAPPENED TODAY?

WHAT POSITIVITY DID I PUT OUT INTO THE WORLD TODAY?

WHAT IS MY FAVORITE MOMENT OF THE DAY?

> "I can't change the direction of the wind, but I can adjust my sails to always reach my destination."
> - Jimmy Dean

WHAT ARE 3 SMALL THINGS I APPRECIATED TODAY?

WHAT ARE MY WINS FOR TODAY?

DESCRIBE TODAY IN 1 WORD.

WHAT ARE MY GOALS FOR TOMORROW?

The Benefits of Self-Compassion and Reframing

Self-compassion is about treating yourself with the same kindness and understanding you'd offer a friend or relative. Think about it: if a friend came to you feeling upset, you wouldn't tell them they're a failure or criticize them for how they feel. You'd probably say something supportive like, "It's okay to feel this way. You're doing your best." That's what self-compassion is—learning to talk to yourself in a way that is gentle and supportive, even when things don't go as planned.

Dr. Kristin Neff*, a leading expert on self-compassion, breaks it down into three parts. First, there's self-kindness, which means being gentle with yourself instead of beating yourself up for every mistake. Second, there's common humanity, which is realizing we all struggle sometimes. You're not alone in feeling anxious or making mistakes—it's part of being human. Third, there's mindfulness, which in this case means noticing your feelings without judging them in the moment. Instead of thinking, "I shouldn't feel this way," mindfulness is, "I'm feeling anxious right now, and that's okay."

One way to practice self-compassion is by learning to reframe. Reframing is about shifting your perspective to see things in a different light. For example, instead of thinking, "I failed," you might say, "I learned something important that will help me next time." It's not about ignoring what did not go well—it's about finding the lesson or opportunity for growth in the experience. Reframing can turn anxious or self-critical thoughts into something more balanced and helpful.

Why is self-compassion so powerful? For starters, it quiets harsh, self-critical thoughts that can cause anxiety. When you're kind to yourself, it's easier to bounce back from challenges because you're not tearing yourself further down. Self-compassion also builds resilience by reminding you mistakes are normal and okay.

*NEFF, K. (2003). Self-Compassion: An Alternative Conceptualization of a Healthy Attitude Toward Oneself. Self and Identity, 2(2), 85–101. https://doi.org/10.1080/15298860309032
Website: https://self-compassion.org

Everyone has hard days, and being kind to yourself during those times can make it easier to keep going.

Here are two simple exercises to get started.

First, write a kind note to yourself, just as if you'd write to a friend who's struggling. What would you say to encourage and comfort them? Second, think about a recent time when you were hard on yourself. Maybe you thought, "I messed everything up."

Now, try to reframe that thought into something more positive or neutral, such as, "I made a mistake, but I can learn from this." These small steps can help you build self-compassion and give yourself the grace you deserve.

FILL EACH DAY WITH

DATE :

BREATHE BEFORE WRITING...

INHALE EXHALE INHALE EXHALE INHALE EXHALE

WHAT ARE 3 GOOD THINGS WHICH HAPPENED TODAY?

WHAT POSITIVITY DID I PUT OUT INTO THE WORLD TODAY?

WHAT IS MY FAVORITE MOMENT OF THE DAY?

> "Life is 10% what happens to us and 90% how we react to it."
> - Charles R. Swindoll

WHAT ARE 3 SMALL THINGS I APPRECIATED TODAY?

WHAT ARE MY WINS FOR TODAY?

DESCRIBE TODAY IN 1 WORD.

WHAT ARE MY GOALS FOR TOMORROW?

Journaling Prompts and Their Benefits for Mental Health

Journaling is a great way to process thoughts, emotions, and experiences. Each prompt serves a specific purpose, helping you explore your feelings, gain clarity, and develop healthier thought patterns. Below is a list of prompts with explanations of their benefits and how they positively impact your mental health.

Gratitude Prompts
- What are three things you're grateful for today?
  - Why it's beneficial: Gratitude shifts your focus from what's wrong to what's going well. It trains your brain to notice the good, thus improving overall mood and resilience.
  - Impact: It encourages a positive mindset and reduces stress.
- Who has made a positive impact on your life, and how?
  - Why it's beneficial: Reflecting on supportive relationships can foster a sense of connection and gratitude for the relationship.
  - Impact: It strengthens emotional bonds and reduces feelings of loneliness.

Self-Reflection Prompts
- What's something you've accomplished recently that you're proud of?
  - Why it's beneficial: Acknowledging achievements builds self-esteem and negates negative self-talk.
  - Impact: It increases confidence and motivation.
- What's one challenge you're currently facing, and what steps can you take to address it?
  - Why it's beneficial: Identifying challenges and solutions encourages problem-solving and reduces overwhelm.
  - Impact: It promotes a sense of control and reduces anxiety.
- What's a lesson you've learned from a mistake you've made?
  - Why it's beneficial: It helps reframe mistakes as opportunities for growth instead of failure.

Exploration and Creativity Prompts
- If you could talk to your past self, what advice would you give yourself?
  - Why it's beneficial: This encourages self-reflection and helps you appreciate how far you've come.
  - Impact: It builds self-awareness and acceptance.
- What would you do if you weren't afraid?
  - Why it's beneficial: It helps you confront fears and imagine possibilities beyond anxiety.
  - Impact: It encourages bold thinking and reduces fear-driven limitations.
- Write about a time when you felt truly at peace. What were you doing, and what made it special?
- Why it's beneficial: Reflecting on peaceful moments helps you identify activities or environments that calm you.
- Impact: It guides you toward creating more peace in your life.

Future-Focused Prompts
- What's one thing you're looking forward to, and why?
  - Why it's beneficial: Anticipating positive experiences can boost mood and motivation.
  - Impact: It encourages optimism and hope.
- What do you want to say to your future self?
  - Why it's beneficial: It creates a sense of accountability and allows you to connect with long-term goals.
  - Impact: It builds motivation and future focus.

Journaling is a tool that meets you where you are. Whether you're reflecting, planning, or just unloading, prompts are designed to help you explore your thoughts and emotions in a safe, supportive way. Over time, you'll notice patterns, discover strengths, and feel more in tune with yourself. Give these prompts a try and watch how they transform your mental health journey!

FILL EACH DAY WITH

DATE :

BREATHE BEFORE WRITING...

INHALE EXHALE INHALE EXHALE INHALE EXHALE

WHAT ARE 3 GOOD THINGS WHICH HAPPENED TODAY?

WHAT POSITIVITY DID I PUT OUT INTO THE WORLD TODAY?

WHAT IS MY FAVORITE MOMENT OF THE DAY?

> "A successful person is one who can lay a firm foundation with the bricks others have thrown at them."
> - David Brinkley

WHAT ARE 3 SMALL THINGS I APPRECIATED TODAY?

WHAT ARE MY WINS FOR TODAY?

DESCRIBE TODAY IN 1 WORD.

WHAT ARE MY GOALS FOR TOMORROW?

Additional Thoughts & Reflection

Additional Thoughts & Reflection

_____
_____
_____
_____
_____
_____
_____
_____
_____
_____
_____
_____
_____
_____
_____
_____
_____
_____
_____
_____
_____
_____
_____

FILL EACH DAY WITH

DATE :

BREATHE BEFORE WRITING...

INHALE EXHALE INHALE EXHALE INHALE EXHALE

WHAT ARE 3 GOOD THINGS WHICH HAPPENED TODAY?

WHAT POSITIVITY DID I PUT OUT INTO THE WORLD TODAY?

WHAT IS MY FAVORITE MOMENT OF THE DAY?

> "The only person you are destined to become is the person you decide to be."
> - Ralph Waldo Emerson

WHAT ARE 3 SMALL THINGS I APPRECIATED TODAY?

WHAT ARE MY WINS FOR TODAY?

DESCRIBE TODAY IN 1 WORD.

WHAT ARE MY GOALS FOR TOMORROW?

Finding CALM in Anxiety

Sometimes, worry feels like a big storm in your head. Your heart beats fast, your thoughts won't stop, and everything feels scary. When this happens, you might not know what to do. That's why I want to share the CALM framework, developed to help with anxiety. CALM stands for Comfort, Anchor, Look at it differently, and Move forward. These four steps can help you feel better when worry takes over.

C is for Comfort

The first step is to remind yourself feeling worried is okay. Everyone feels this way at times. Anxiety is just your brain trying to help, even if it doesn't feel that way. When you feel worried, tell yourself, "It's okay to feel this way—lots of people do." Just like your body gets cold in winter, your mind reacts to stress with worry; it's a natural reaction. Instead of trying to make it go away fast, let yourself know it's normal.

A is for Anchor

When worry distracts you, you need something to hold onto. That's called an anchor. Anchoring is finding a way to feel safe and keeping yourself in the right now. You can take deep breaths, press your feet into the ground, or hold something soft; use any of the grounding techniques discussed earlier. You can also look around and name five things you see. Tell yourself, "Let's find a way to feel safe right now." Anchors help you stay in the moment instead of getting lost in fear.

L is for Look at it differently

Worry can create scary ideas in your mind. You might think, "I will mess up," or "Something bad will happen." But what if you changed that idea? Instead of thinking, "I can't do this," ask, "What's one good way to see this?" Maybe this challenge will help you grow. Maybe this feeling means you care about something. Instead of fear, think of anxiety as a helper. Say, "This feeling can help me learn and grow."

M is for Move forward

The last step is to remember getting better takes time. There's no magic trick, but every time you try, you get stronger. Even if you still feel worried, practicing these steps helps. Celebrate small wins—maybe you spoke up in class, tried something new, or handled a hard moment. If you have a bad day, be kind to yourself. Say, "Getting better takes time—I am learning every day." Moving forward isn't about stopping worry forever—it's about learning how to handle it.

When you feel worried, remember CALM: Comfort yourself, Anchor yourself in the present, Look at things in a new way, and Move forward. The more you practice, the easier it gets. Worry doesn't have to be in charge—you can find your calm no matter what happens.

FILL EACH DAY WITH

DATE :

BREATHE BEFORE WRITING...

INHALE EXHALE INHALE EXHALE INHALE EXHALE

WHAT ARE 3 GOOD THINGS WHICH HAPPENED TODAY?

WHAT POSITIVITY DID I PUT OUT INTO THE WORLD TODAY?

WHAT IS MY FAVORITE MOMENT OF THE DAY?

> "Challenges are what make life interesting and overcoming them is what makes life meaningful."
> - Joshua J. Marine

WHAT ARE 3 SMALL THINGS I APPRECIATED TODAY?

WHAT ARE MY WINS FOR TODAY?

DESCRIBE TODAY IN 1 WORD.

WHAT ARE MY GOALS FOR TOMORROW?

Breaking the Anxiety Cycle

Anxiety can feel like an endless loop, like a song stuck on repeat that you can't turn off. This loop is called the anxiety cycle, and understanding it is the first step to gaining control over it. The anxiety cycle works like this: You experience a trigger; something that makes you feel nervous or uncertain. Your brain sees it as a threat, and your body reacts with fear or worry. This leads to avoidance: pulling away from the situation, distracting yourself, or shutting down. In the moment, avoiding what makes you anxious might bring relief, but over time, it actually makes anxiety stronger. The next time that trigger appears, your brain remembers, "This is scary!" and the cycle starts all over again.

To break the anxiety cycle, you first need to recognize it. Think about the last time you felt anxious. What set it off? What did you feel in your body? Did your heart race? Did you feel dizzy or overwhelmed? What did you do next—did you face it or try to avoid it? These questions help you identify patterns in your anxiety. Once you see the cycle, you can start to change it. Instead of avoiding the situation, try leaning into it slowly. Remind yourself, "I've felt this before, and I got through it." Small steps, like using breathing techniques, grounding exercises, or challenging negative thoughts, can help you take back control.

While everyone feels anxious sometimes, how do you know if your anxiety is normal or if it might be at a clinical level? Ask yourself these questions:
* Does my anxiety stop me from doing everyday things, like going to school, work, or social events?
* Do I avoid situations or people because of my anxiety?
* Does my anxiety feel out of proportion? Do I have physical symptoms, like headaches, stomachaches, or lack of sleep, because of my worry?
* Does my anxiety last for weeks or months, even when things seem okay?

If you answered "yes" to these questions, you might be experiencing an anxiety disorder. This isn't something to be ashamed of, and you're not alone—many people struggle with anxiety at a clinical level. If your anxiety feels overwhelming, it may be time to reach out for help. A therapist or doctor can work with you to find strategies to make anxiety more manageable. Seeking help doesn't mean something is wrong with you—it means you're taking steps to care for yourself, just like you would if you had a physical illness.

It's also important to know anxiety can co-occur with other mental health conditions, such as depression, ADHD, or PTSD. Sometimes, anxiety is just one piece of a bigger picture. If you find yourself feeling hopeless, struggling to focus, experiencing mood swings, or having frequent flashbacks of past events, it's worth talking to a professional who can help you figure out what's going on. Mental health is complex, and getting the right support can make a world of difference.

As we wrap up this journey through understanding anxiety, take a moment to reflect. Think about where you were when you started learning about anxiety and where you are now. Ask yourself:

- What have I learned about my own anxiety patterns?
- What tools or techniques have helped me the most?
- What challenges still feel difficult, and how can I work through them?

FILL EACH DAY WITH

DATE :

BREATHE BEFORE WRITING...

INHALE EXHALE INHALE EXHALE INHALE EXHALE

WHAT ARE 3 GOOD THINGS WHICH HAPPENED TODAY?

WHAT POSITIVITY DID I PUT OUT INTO THE WORLD TODAY?

WHAT IS MY FAVORITE MOMENT OF THE DAY?

> "I have learned over the years that when one's mind is made up, this diminishes fear."
> - Rosa Parks

WHAT ARE 3 SMALL THINGS I APPRECIATED TODAY?

WHAT ARE MY WINS FOR TODAY?

DESCRIBE TODAY IN 1 WORD.

WHAT ARE MY GOALS FOR TOMORROW?

30-Day Habit Log

New Habit:

_____

Why is this important to me?

_____

_____

My Strengths:

_____

My Weaknesses:

_____

Rewards:

_____

Let's do this!

How did it go?

_____

_____

What did I learn?

_____

_____

Rate how hard this habit is   ☆ ☆ ☆ ☆ ☆

Monthly Habit Tracker

1	2	3	4	5 MEETING	6
7	8	9	10	11	12
13	14	15	16	17	18
19	20	21	22	23	24
25	26	27 DON'T 4GET	28	29	30

Notes

Habit Tracker

FILL EACH DAY WITH

DATE :

Positivity

BREATHE BEFORE WRITING...

INHALE EXHALE INHALE EXHALE INHALE EXHALE

WHAT ARE 3 GOOD THINGS WHICH HAPPENED TODAY?

WHAT POSITIVITY DID I PUT OUT INTO THE WORLD TODAY?

WHAT IS MY FAVORITE MOMENT OF THE DAY?

> "The only way to have a good day is to start it with a positive attitude."
> - Unknown

WHAT ARE 3 SMALL THINGS I APPRECIATED TODAY?

WHAT ARE MY WINS FOR TODAY?

DESCRIBE TODAY IN 1 WORD.

WHAT ARE MY GOALS FOR TOMORROW?

Dear Future Me

A Letter of Hope and Encouragement

Take a few minutes to picture your future self—maybe thirty days, six months, a year, or even five years down the road. Where do you see yourself? What challenges do you hope to overcome? What dreams do you want to have brought to life? Use this space to write a letter to your future self, sharing your thoughts, feelings, and hopes. Offer words of encouragement and wisdom that will inspire you when you read this letter later on.

To help you get started, here are some phrases you can use to start writing:

1. Reflect on Today:
   - "Right now, I'm feeling …"
   - "Some things I'm working on or struggling with are …"

2. What You Hope For:
   - "In the next year, I hope you have …"
   - "Remember, even when things get tough, you are …"

3. Words of Encouragement:
   - "You've come so far in …"
   - "I'm proud of you for …"

4. Goals and Dreams:
   - "I hope by now you have achieved …"
   - "Don't lose sight of …"

5. Personal Growth:
   - "I hope you've learned to …"
   - "Remember to be kind to yourself when …"

6. Gratitude and Positivity:
   - "Take time to appreciate …"
   - "You've created more peace and joy by …"

7. Closing Thoughts:
- "No matter what happens, always remember …"
- "You're capable of …"

Here's an example of a letter:

Hey Future Me,

Right now, I'm feeling a mix of hope and uncertainty as I work through some challenges with anxiety. I'm trying to be more present, take things one day at a time, and build healthier habits. I hope by the time you read this, you've found more peace and confidence in yourself.

You've already come so far, and I hope you keep showing up for yourself. Even when things feel overwhelming, remember how resilient you are. I hope you've continued to grow, stay true to your values, and find joy in those everyday moments that matter most.

Keep pushing toward your dreams, no matter how big or small. You've got this. I'm proud of the progress you've made and the strength you've shown. You've already achieved so much, and I know there's so much more to come.

Don't forget to celebrate your victories, no matter how small they seem. I believe in you, and I know you're capable of amazing things.

With love and gratitude,
Me

Reflection:
When you're done writing, tuck your letter away somewhere safe. Write a date on it—maybe six months or a year from now. When the time comes, revisit your letter to see how much you've grown, what you've achieved, and to remind yourself of the hope and strength that's always been within you.

FILL EACH DAY WITH

DATE :

BREATHE BEFORE WRITING...

INHALE EXHALE INHALE EXHALE INHALE EXHALE

WHAT ARE 3 GOOD THINGS WHICH HAPPENED TODAY?

WHAT POSITIVITY DID I PUT OUT INTO THE WORLD TODAY?

WHAT IS MY FAVORITE MOMENT OF THE DAY?

"Success is not the key to happiness. Happiness is the key to success. If you love what you are doing, you will be successful."
- Albert Schweitzer

WHAT ARE 3 SMALL THINGS I APPRECIATED TODAY?

WHAT ARE MY WINS FOR TODAY?

DESCRIBE TODAY IN 1 WORD.

WHAT ARE MY GOALS FOR TOMORROW?

Additional Thoughts & Reflection

_____
_____
_____
_____
_____
_____
_____
_____
_____
_____
_____
_____
_____
_____
_____
_____
_____
_____
_____
_____
_____
_____
_____
_____

Additional Thoughts & Reflection

_____
_____
_____
_____
_____
_____
_____
_____
_____
_____
_____
_____
_____
_____
_____
_____
_____
_____
_____
_____
_____

FILL EACH DAY WITH

DATE :

BREATHE BEFORE WRITING...

INHALE

EXHALE

INHALE

EXHALE

INHALE

EXHALE

WHAT ARE 3 GOOD THINGS WHICH HAPPENED TODAY?

WHAT POSITIVITY DID I PUT OUT INTO THE WORLD TODAY?

WHAT IS MY FAVORITE MOMENT OF THE DAY?

> "If you don't like something, change it. If you can't change it, change your attitude."
> - Maya Angelou

WHAT ARE 3 SMALL THINGS I APPRECIATED TODAY?

WHAT ARE MY WINS FOR TODAY?

DESCRIBE TODAY IN 1 WORD.

WHAT ARE MY GOALS FOR TOMORROW?

Time to Stir the Lemonade

Week 4: Overcoming Limiting Beliefs

Limiting Belief	Source of the Limiting Belief	Examples Where the Limiting Belief was not True

Additional Thoughts & Reflection

Additional Thoughts & Reflection

Some Habit Options

- Start your day without your phone
- Move your body
- Make your bed
- Drink water first thing in the morning
- Create a simple morning routine
- Practice deep listening
- Limit screen time before bed
- Do something creative
- Limit caffeine intake
- Use affirmations
- Practice small acts of kindness
- Keep a worry journal
- Set daily intentions
- Limit doomscrolling
- Create a bedtime routine
- Schedule breaks throughout the day
- Journal before bed
- Declutter your space
- Increase your water consumption
- Meal plan/prep weekly
- Meditate or practice mindfulness
- Reach out to friends/relatives weekly
- Engage in preventive self-care
- Make your bed
- Set aside time for budgeting/financial planning

Looking Back to Move Forward

Thoughts to Reflect On

- If you were to ask someone else about your ability to manage your ability to manage your anxiety in the past month what do you think they would say at the beginning of the month versus now?
- What is something positive that happened to you this month?
- What strengths have helped you overcome challenges in the past month?
- How have you grown as a person in the last month?
- Who in your life made you feel seen and supported, and why?
- How have you show yourself kindness this past month?
- What is a challenge you addressed that once seemed impossible?
- What activities brought you joy or helped you feel calm this month?
- How can you reframe a current worry into a more positive thought?
- What is one act of kindness you did for someone else this past month?
- What are three things in your environment that make you feel safe and at ease?
- What does self-care mean to you, and how will you prioritize it in the future?

Additional Thoughts & Reflection

Self Re-Assessment

- [ ] _____
- [ ] _____
- [ ] _____
- [ ] _____
- [ ] _____
- [ ] _____
- [ ] _____
- [ ] _____
- [ ] _____
- [ ] _____

- [ ] _____
- [ ] _____
- [ ] _____
- [ ] _____
- [ ] _____
- [ ] _____
- [ ] _____
- [ ] _____
- [ ] _____

I am proud of myself because...

_____

_____

_____

Something I now see differently is...

_____

_____

_____

Stay Connected

Thank you for joining me on this journey of self-discovery and growth. Your story doesn't end here, and I'd love to stay connected as you continue to thrive. For more resources, tips, and inspiration, be sure to follow me on social media:

LinkedIn:

Facebook:

Instagram:

If you're looking for additional support or want to dive deeper into these practices, check out the online companion guide! Simply scan the QR code below to access it:

Remember, you're never alone on this path. Keep showing up for yourself, and I'll be right there to cheer you on!

With gratitude,

Whitney Coleman. LICSW, LCSW-C